FACING THE ODDS: THE HEALING POWER OF POKER AND THE BATTLE WITH PTSD

SHAUN COLQUHOUN

In the bustling poker rooms and silent aftermaths of battle, Shaun Colquhoun navigated two disparate worlds. One, a realm of calculated risks and bluffs; the other, an arena of visceral fears and haunting memories. Yet, when these worlds converged, an unexpected journey of healing began.

"Facing the Odds" takes you through the raw, emotional landscapes of Shaun's life. As a soldier returning from the harrowing terrains of Afghanistan, the weight of PTSD pressed heavily on him. But in the vibrant, unpredictable world of poker, Shaun found more than just a game. He discovered a refuge, a mental escape, and an unconventional therapy.

Walk with Shaun as he recounts those high-stake nights at the table that paralleled his high-stakes battle with trauma. From the neon lights of Las Vegas casinos to intense therapy rooms, this memoir delves deep into the complexities of the human spirit. It's a testament to resilience, friendship, and the unexpected places one finds healing.

Shaun's journey reveals that life isn't solely about the hand you're dealt, but the courage with which you play it. And in the confluence of cards and combat, he offers a profound message: In the face of adversity, sometimes our most powerful ally is a challenge itself.

"In life, as in poker, courage isn't holding onto something when the odds are against you. It's the strength to let go, learn, and return to the table stronger than before."

Shaun Colquhoun

Las Vegas, NV   FacingTheOdds.com

SHARED STORIES
ONE PERSPECTIVE

In 'Facing the Odds: The Healing Power of Poker and the Battle with PTSD,' the narratives that unfurl are a harmonious blend of individual experiences, shared by countless soldiers yet masterfully woven into a singular, poignant perspective. While many of these stories spring from Shaun's own journey, several have been entrusted to him by comrades who sought anonymity, their tales too raw and personal to be named. To honor their truths and give weight to their battles, Shaun recounts the entire tale through his own lens, imbuing the collective experiences with the depth and emotion of a personal memoir.

"In the intricate dance of life, sometimes it's not the cards we're dealt, but how we play them, that defines our resilience."

PROLOGUE

In a world constantly on the move, in the hustle and undying rustle of everyday life, we find solace in the strangest of places. This book, much more than a tale of survival, is a journey through the labyrinth of the human mind, the battles fought within, and the redemption found in unexpected quarters. It's a narrative penned down to inspire, inform, and ignite a beacon of hope for those navigating the treacherous waters of trauma, loss, and recovery.

Before the call of duty whispered in my ear, my life was a chaotic symphony of constant movement, devoid of stability. I was a running prodigy, threading my way through cross country tracks, racing not just against time but against the shadows of an alcoholic home, against the vivid memories of my father's tragic demise in the murky world of drugs. The memories were a labyrinth, but running was the thread that led me out of it, towards a glimpse of normalcy.

When the golden gates of scholarship opened for me, they were only half-ajar, the remnants barred by financial constraints. College seemed like a distant dream until the military became the bridge to it. The choice was more out of desperation than aspiration, a gamble in the recruiting center at Hollywood blvd, and the dice rolled out to be 11b– infantryman. The wager was not just in service but in the very essence of life, in the face of relentless danger, a path littered with the remnants of friends lost and a self rediscovered in the haunting echo of gunshots.

It was in the silent whispers of the Afghani winds, the rhythmic thump of the helicopters, and the silent tears for fallen friends like Sgt. Johnston, that the seeds of my battle within were sown—a battle labeled as PTSD. The nightmares were no longer confined to the realm of sleep; they bled into the daylight, morphed into innocuous objects, a piece of trash, a hum of an air conditioner, shadows in the corner of my eye.

This book was born from the ashes of those battles, from the realization that the ghosts of the past could be faced, not just through conventional therapy but through the shuffle of cards, the clink of poker chips, and the camaraderie around a table. It's a testament to the transformative power of poker, a game that became a beacon of light in the encompassing darkness, a game that held my hand through the landmines of my mind, allowing me to navigate through them, to live beyond them.

My journey with poker was a random stumble, a friend's invitation into the secretive, intimate world of underground poker rooms, a world vibrating with the melody of shuffling chips and whispered strategies. It was a sanctuary where my demons were silent spectators, their voices drowned in the friendly banter and the rustle of cards. Poker was not just a game; it was a canvas where I painted my recovery, a teacher that schooled me in the art of living, and a friend that listened when the world around was deafened by its chaos.

The narrative ahead is more than just my story; it's a bridge between worlds, a conversation starter between those plagued by the shadows of their mind and those oblivious to them. It's a hand extended in understanding and support to those whose lives are puppeteered by PTSD, to those who look at the smiling faces around them and see the masks of unshed tears and unsaid words. It's for the families, walking on the tightrope of love and helplessness, looking for a ray of hope in the enveloping darkness.

The objective is not just to inform but to make this journey relatable to everyone, to create a symphony that resonates with every soul, whether bathed in the light of knowledge or shrouded in the shadows of ignorance about PTSD, poker, or military life. It's a dance of words, a blend of the playful and the serious, the light and the dark, creating a melody that is the echo of every soul in pain, every soul in recovery.

This journey is an ode to the resilience of the human spirit, to the silent warriors battling their invisible enemies, and to the unseen hands of support, guiding them through their darkest hours. It's a tribute to the transformational power of the mind, to the magic woven by the hands of friendship and the strength found in the most unexpected places. So, walk with me through this journey, through the pages of my life, my battles, my victories, and my losses, and let's paint the world with the colors of hope, resilience, and recovery. Welcome to my symphony, my labyrinth, my redemption. Welcome to my story.

Chapter 1

A SOLDIER'S MIND: THE ONSET OF PTSD

It was a night like any other. The warm, shimmering lights of Pechanga Casino in Temecula, CA, were inviting, promising a refuge from reality, a place where the torments of the past could be forgotten, if only for a little while. My best friend Adam and I found ourselves immersed in the enticing world of chance, reveling in the little joys and the camaraderie of our youth. The cards were in our favor, a rare winning streak in blackjack filling our pockets with more than just hopes. But the real gamble was not at the tables—it was within my mind.

In the sanctuary of my luxurious hotel room, a battle was raging. The hum of the air conditioner, a monotonous whomp, whomp, whomp, became the rotor blades of a Chinook, skimming above the desolate, embattled terrains of Helmand, Afghanistan. The illusion was so powerful, so vivid, that the danger felt imminent, the fear, real. A spray of enemy bullets rained through our hull, each thunk a stark reminder of my vulnerability, of the fragility of life amidst the chaos of war.

In this half-dream, half-reality state, I was no longer Shaun, the young guy goofing off at a casino; I was a soldier, my senses heightened, adrenaline coursing through my veins, preparing me for the warfare I was so familiar with. Every bump, every sound was a reminder of the helplessness and the surreal acceptance of the fatal possibilities. As the Chinook landed and we disembarked in haste, I was jolted awake, my bed a drenched remnant of the turmoil within.

The battlefield had imprinted itself on my mind, transforming my everyday life into a labyrinth of triggers. Nightmares morphed into daymares; past became present. The act of picking up fallen French fries at McDonald's transported me to a grim memory of collecting a friend's severed fingers. A simple splinter was not just a piece of wood piercing my skin, but a painful reminder of pulling out bone fragments from my own body.

Every seemingly mundane element became a potential trigger, popcorn, a driving hazard, even a harmless McDonald's bag discarded on the road. A drive through Stanford on the way to the golf course years later was disrupted by the sight of a piece of trash, a seemingly meaningless object to any passerby. To me, it was a potential IED, leading to a surge of panic, swerving, and shouts of warning, followed by the suffocating realization that there was no explosion, no enemy fire, no casualties–

just me, Shaun, inches away from a fence, surrounded by the serene beauty of Stanford's trees.

This is the relentless struggle of living with PTSD, where the past is not just a collection of memories but a constant companion, shaping, defining, and often disrupting the present. In this chapter, we will explore the unyielding grip of PTSD, the invisible wounds carried by soldiers, and the journey toward understanding, acceptance, and ultimately, healing.

The war was over; at least, that's what they told me. The tangible, physical combat had ended the moment my boots left the arid soil of Afghanistan. However, the mental warfare lingered, and in many ways, it was just beginning.

My days morphed into a continuous struggle, an effort to separate reality from haunting memories. Every mundane activity became a battlefield where I fought to maintain a semblance of normalcy. Life was no longer simple; the experiences overseas had woven a complex, often debilitating web of triggers, reminders, and flashbacks.

In that convoluted space between the past and the present, my mind was entangled within its own enigmatic war zone. Each day brought new battles, different adversaries. For those around me, my actions might have seemed erratic, unpredictable, and on certain days, even unfathomable. But inside my mind, every reaction was a learned response, a survival mechanism developed in a place where discarded litter could be a concealed threat, and familiar faces could be lost in an instant.

Conversations were punctuated with awkward pauses, as my mind occasionally traveled back to the treacherous terrains of Helmand. I would be there, amidst friends or family, physically present but mentally miles away, sifting through the debris of memories best left forgotten. Their voices would fade into the distant echo of gunfire, laughter morphing into cries of pain and despair from wounded comrades.

Understanding and addressing PTSD was like trying to contain a tempest in a teapot. Initially, the coping mechanisms I employed were evasive, a mix of denial and dismissal. "I'm fine," I'd often declare, even when sleepless nights and anxiety-ridden days painted a starkly different picture.

Adam, ever the steadfast friend, bore witness to my struggles, often without fully comprehending the depth of my internal turmoil. How could he? How could anyone who hadn't been plunged into that abyss truly understand the ghostly remnants that haunted my every waking moment?

It was during one such episode, a seemingly inconsequential moment marred by an invisible yet omnipresent enemy, that Adam gently nudged me toward seeking help. He had seen the distant look in my eyes, recognized the subtle flinch at a sudden noise, and understood that beneath the tough exterior was a friend grappling with specters from the past.

And so, the journey towards understanding, acceptance, and healing began. But it was not linear, nor was it predictable. Treatments, counseling, and various therapies opened a Pandora's box of emotions and memories, some so deeply buried that their surfacing was akin to ripping a bandage off a festering wound. Vulnerability, fear, and grief were juxtaposed with moments of clarity and progress.

In the coming pages, we will navigate through these experiences, exploring the labyrinthine mind of a soldier tormented by the echoes of warfare. We'll delve deeper into coping mechanisms, both constructive and destructive, as well as the various treatments and therapies that offer a glimmer of hope amidst the chaos.

As days turned into nights and weeks into months, the spectral grip of Helmand's memories didn't loosen; it merely transformed, coiling around each experience with a stealthy, insidious persistence. My mind, once a haven, became a staging ground for relentless battles between the man I was and the soldier I had become.

Support groups became an integral part of my journey towards healing. Within the confines of those walls, I encountered others who, like me, were combatting their own internal demons. The first few sessions were like walking through a minefield. Each shared story, every uttered word, held the potential to detonate memories that I'd spent countless hours attempting to suppress.

When Mike, a Marine with kind eyes and a subdued demeanor, shared his story of losing his best friend to an IED, my heart plunged into an abyss of shared pain and kinship. His words, while unveiling his own agony, unknowingly tapped into my suppressed torment, briefly blurring the lines between his grief and mine.

Despite the overwhelming emotions, there was an unspoken bond in that room, a mutual understanding that we were all wayfarers on a similar journey through the undulating terrains of trauma and recovery. It provided a sliver of comfort, a gentle reminder that I was not alone in this desolate space between what was and what could be.

The difficulty of those sessions was tangible, yet they brought with them an unexpected relief. The emotional purging, while draining, allowed me to navigate through the pain rather than constantly sidestepping it.

A particular breakthrough occurred on a day enveloped by the gentle caress of a spring breeze, an odd juxtaposition to the emotional storm brewing within. My therapist, Dr. Anderson, gently probed into the fortified recesses of my memories, nudging me towards confronting the guilt that had imperceptibly yet irrevocably entwined itself around my psyche.

It was the story of a young Afghan girl, no older than my niece, whose life was forever altered by the crossfire of conflicting ideals and artillery. Her face, a mosaic of innocence and suffering, haunted me, propelling me into a vortex of guilt and self-loathing. Was I, like the enemy I fought, a harbinger of her pain and loss?

Dr. Anderson, with a gentle yet firm resolve, guided me through this turbulent sea of self-recrimination, helping me to acknowledge the complexity of my emotions without being completely subsumed by them. We dissected the guilt, the pain, and the immense burden of surviving when so many did not.

Unpacking these emotions was akin to sifting through the wreckage left in the wake of a storm - chaotic, heart-wrenching, yet necessary. Healing, I realized, was not a destination but a continuous journey, fraught with its own challenges and moments of despair, yet illuminated by sporadic bursts of hope and self-discovery.

Through the process, Adam remained a steadfast beacon of friendship and understanding. He became a silent observer of my internal battles, never prying, yet always present. His unwavering support was a testament to the unspoken bond forged through years of friendship and shared experiences.

The path towards recovery, towards reclaiming one's self from the abyss of PTSD, is neither linear nor predictable. It meanders through moments of darkness and light, pain and relief, chaos and serenity. And so, my journey continues...

My steps towards recovery weren't a solo journey but rather a collective endeavor, involving family, friends, and professionals, each playing a pivotal role in navigating through the entwined paths of trauma and healing. The solace found in those support groups, the sanctuary provided by my loved ones, and the professional aid from therapists, became the trinity upon which my recovery was anchored.

Treatment began with cognitive-behavioral therapy (CBT), where Dr. Anderson and I delved into the labyrinth of my mind, gently sifting through the traumatic memories, dismantling them piece by piece in a safe and controlled environment. Each session was a step towards disarming the power these memories wielded, turning them from tormenting flashbacks into narratives that I could control and understand.

Simultaneously, Eye Movement Desensitization and Reprocessing (EMDR) became a pivotal part of my therapeutic journey. It was a peculiar experience at first, my eyes following Dr. Anderson's fingers back and forth, as we unearthed and reprocessed traumatic memories. The process aimed to change the way those memories were stored in my brain, stripping them of their emotional charge and placing them into a coherent narrative that was easier to accept and understand.

But therapy wasn't the only sanctuary. I found a semblance of peace in the art of mindfulness and meditation, techniques taught to me by a veteran named Lucy during a group session. She spoke eloquently about the present moment being a refuge, and gradually, through practice, I began to find brief respites from my tormenting thoughts as I learned to anchor myself in the here and now.

Adam, ever the pillar of support, found solace in joining me during these mindful moments. We'd often find ourselves seated amidst nature, allowing the serenity of the present moment to envelop our beings, providing a temporary respite from the chaos within. His unspoken understanding and shared silence became a comforting presence, a gentle acknowledgment of shared pain and mutual healing.

I also explored expressive therapies - converting the internal chaos into tangible forms through writing and art. My words became a medium through which pain was transformed into stories, while colors and shapes on canvas mirrored the tumultuous emotions within, offering a visual representation of my internal world. It was therapeutic, to express without judgment, to create without constraints, allowing the suppressed emotions a safe passage out of my being.

My nightly rituals became infused with a combination of these coping mechanisms - a silent prayer, a moment of mindfulness, and a gentle acknowledgment of the progress made. The nightmares, while not entirely dissipated, began to lose their crippling power as my mind gradually learned to dissociate fear and panic from those haunting memories.

As the chapter of recovery continued to unfold, I began to understand that the journey wasn't about erasing the past, but learning to live with it in a way that it didn't consume my present. It was about accepting the coexistence of pain and peace, understanding that healing is not the absence of wounds but learning to carry them without being encumbered.

The path ahead was far from linear. It would meander through moments of relapse and recovery, each step forward accompanied by the shadows of the past. Yet, with each passing day, those shadows became less intimidating, gradually morphing from monstrous entities into solemn reminders of a past that no longer held the reins to my present.

And so, I step forward, not with an aim to forget, but to remember without pain, to carry forward not just the scars but also the lessons they brought with them. My name is Shaun, and this is my perpetual journey from the battlefields of Afghanistan to the internal skirmishes within, a journey towards healing, acceptance, and eventual peace.

Chapter 2

DISCOVERING THE DECK: A NEW BEGINNING

There's a saying that sometimes life presents you with unexpected gifts when you least expect them. For me, that unexpected gift came in the form of playing cards, and with it, the captivating world of poker.

It began in Myrtle Beach, South Carolina. Joe Smith, a close friend and someone I held deep respect for, invited me to an experience that would later play a transformative role in my life. I was accustomed to the unpredictable nature of things, having served in the military, but this night was unpredictability of a different kind. Joe had spoken very little about what to expect, and as we approached the façade of an abandoned strip mall, my intrigue piqued.

The entrance process felt straight out of a heist movie. Cameras, blackout doors, the showing of our torsos, ensuring we weren't armed or posing any threat. Then, as the heavy steel doors conceded, a sensory shift overcame me - the rich symphony of poker chips being shuffled, the comforting hum of conversation, and the rhythmic dance of cards being dealt. I was mesmerized. The air was electric with anticipation, camaraderie, and competition.

The room was bathed in dim lighting, enhancing the clandestine atmosphere. I noted the three poker tables, each surrounded by players deeply engrossed in the game, and a pool table occupying the central space. Every seat was taken, every eye calculating, every hand silently conversing its strategy.

However, what stood out the most was the camaraderie. Nearly everyone there was from the Army. The understanding and solidarity amongst them were palpable. In this covert haven, ranks faded, and the shared love for the game reigned supreme. As newcomers, Joe and I were welcomed with open arms. Their generosity extended beyond mere pleasantries; they were eager to help a novice like me understand the intricacies of the game.

That evening was a sensory and intellectual treat. The game's nuances, the calculated risks, the strategy, the bluffing - it was a ballet of the mind. Poker became an oasis, drawing me away from the haunting memories of the battlefield, even if just momentarily. It was more than a game; it was a mental exercise that honed my focus and decision-making. The unpredictability of each hand mirrored life's uncertainties, teaching me to play with the cards I was dealt, both literally and metaphorically.

Poker also provided a sense of community. The game's social nature meant that I wasn't just playing cards; I was connecting, sharing stories, laughing at jokes, and reveling in the mutual respect and understanding that only soldiers could offer each other. This underground poker room became more than just a place to play; it was a sanctuary where the past's burdens eased, replaced by the thrill of the present hand and the company of those who understood.

In the rhythmic shuffle of cards and the strategic dance of the game, I found a balm for my mind's turmoil. It was a diversion, yes, but also a new beginning. An unexpected chapter where I learned to play, strategize, connect, and most importantly, heal.

Discovering Strategy and Mindfulness

The initial rustle of the poker chips, the stealthy glance of the players, and the mystery embedded in every dealt hand weren't just parts of a game to me. They slowly unfurled as metaphors for life, strategy, and surprisingly, healing.

In those initial days at the poker table in Myrtle Beach, I was a sponge, absorbing the nuances and subtleties of the game. The intricate balance between risk and reward, the art of reading opponents, and the disciplined restraint required in every move - all of it mirrored the complexities I'd navigated during my time in the Army. Only here, in this dimly lit room, the stakes were different, perhaps a bit friendlier, yet the thrill and strategy were remarkably similar.

The benefit of poker to my mind was somewhat unexpected but remarkably profound. With each game, my focus shifted from the perturbing memories and flashbacks of the battlefield to the immediate present - the cards in my hand, the expressions on my opponents' faces, and the stack of chips that ebbed and flowed with each round.

The game demanded a mental agility and emotional neutrality that unwittingly drew me away from the recurring pangs of traumatic recollections. The need to stay present, to strategize each move, to maintain a poker face amidst the turmoil of a good or bad hand, anchored me firmly in the moment, providing a respite from the haunting memories that often clouded my mind.

One particular evening, as a new hand was dealt and the familiar faces around the table engaged in lighthearted banter, I felt a surprising sense of serenity. The cards in my hand, a combination of possibilities and strategies, served as a subtle reminder - life too, was a hand that had been dealt to me, and perhaps, just perhaps, I could learn to play this hand wisely.

The strategic component of poker was curiously therapeutic. I found comfort in the predictability of the rules and the unpredictability of the hands dealt. There was solace in knowing that while the hand was out of my control, how I played it was firmly within my grasp. It was this duality, this blend of fate and strategy, that gradually began to seep into my daily life.

With each shuffle, deal, and bet, I noticed a quietening within, a subtle distance forming between the haunting memories of war and the peaceful present. The immediate need to focus on my hand, to strategize, to remain one step ahead, provided a mental occupation that had been sorely missing.

I began to notice that the hypervigilance, that ever-present tension that had tightly coiled within me since Afghanistan, had loosened its grip slightly. My nights were a tad more peaceful, my reactions to triggering events slightly subdued, and in the faces of my fellow players - my fellow soldiers - I saw reflections of my own journey.

Poker, while seemingly a mere game, became a tool for mindfulness, an unexpected form of therapy that allowed me to step away from the turbulent tides of PTSD, into moments of calm and strategy. It wasn't a cure, but it was a welcome respite, an ally in my ongoing battle against the persistent echoes of war.

Learning from the Loses

The underbelly of the poker room became a sanctuary, an odd haven where the camaraderie of fellow players - soldiers like me - provided a comforting constancy. And the intricate dance of poker, with its highs and lows, began to parallel the very experiences that echoed through my everyday life.

One evening, nestled amongst familiar faces and the rhythmic hum of shuffled cards, I found myself dealt a hand that, under normal circumstances, would elicit a subtle, triumphant smirk - a pair of Aces. The best starting hand in poker, a hand that brought with it an expectancy, a silent prediction of victory. My pulse quickened slightly, and the metaphorical armor I had built around myself thickened, preparing for a battle I was sure to win.

As the rounds progressed, my chips slid confidently into the pot, each bet a reaffirmation of the perceived strength of my hand. My mind, typically a tempest of memories and flashbacks, was sharply focussed, tethered to the present by the crisp cards within my grip.

However, poker, much like life, is unpredictable.

As the final cards were revealed and hands were laid bare, my Aces, once mighty and seemingly invincible, crumbled in the face of a humbling straight flush, skillfully wielded by an opponent. The chips, once proudly amassed before me, meandered away, and I was left with an unexpected void, a sting of loss that was simultaneously familiar and new.

Yet, in this loss, a curious realization blossomed.

Much like the strongest of soldiers can be felled, the mightiest hands in poker can be defeated. It was a poignant reminder that strength is not merely determined by an auspicious beginning or inherent power but is shaped and refined by adaptability, strategy, and an acceptance of the unpredictability of the play - or life's unfolding.

The pair of Aces, once a symbol of impending victory, transformed into a metaphor that would subtly permeate my perspective, both at the table and beyond. It became evident that sometimes, the most formidable starts do not guarantee triumph. Sometimes, even amidst the seemingly assured victory, one must be prepared for loss, for change, and most importantly, for adaptation.

Poker was no longer just a game. It was a mental exercise, a cognitive dance that required a melding of strategy and acceptance, of risk and retreat. This mental diversion, born amidst chips and cards, became a gentle guiding force, redirecting the energies that once were engulfed by the haunting memories of war towards a path of mindfulness and strategic thinking.

Through poker, through every hand dealt, bet placed, and pot lost or won, my mind engaged in a novel form of therapy, a self-prescribed antidote to the chaos that PTSD had sown within. Every loss, every victory became a lesson, not just in the game, but in the management of my own mental and emotional landscapes.

And so, as the cards continued to be dealt and hands continued to be played, my journey of healing, of discovery through the decks and chips, forged ahead, one hand at a time. Each game, whether crowned with victory or humbled by defeat, etched into my path a reminder - that life, much like poker, is played not by the hands we are dealt, but by how we play them.

Finding Calm in Chaos

In the clandestine cocoon of the poker room, amidst the rhapsody of riffling chips and murmured strategy, I found a paradoxical peace within the chaos of cards and stakes. The table became a battlefield of a different kind, where I, Shaun, waged wars not against physical adversaries or the haunting specters of my past but against probabilities, bluffs, and the ever-looming specter of chance.

Poker, with its potent blend of strategy and luck, became an intriguing mirror to life itself. It offered a controlled chaos, a storm that could be navigated with skill, intuition, and a dash of daring. I found myself anchored by the mental rigor poker demanded, even as it mimicked the unpredictability and twists of life outside the warmly lit room.

One memorable evening, as the stakes rose and the atmosphere thickened with palpable tension, I found myself locked into a particularly high-stakes hand. My palms, steady even in the unpredictable terrains of Afghanistan, betrayed a slight tremor, barely noticeable beneath the heavy gaze of my fellow players.

The hand was strong, not unbeatable but substantial, an enticing allure that teased at the possibility of victory. And so, with a steadying breath, I pushed forward a sizable stack of chips, my commitment to the hand laid bare amidst the sea of colors before me.

My opponent, a seasoned player with eyes that revealed nothing, calmly met my bet, his own stack joining the growing mountain in the pot.

As the final card, the river, was smoothly placed by the dealer, a quiet gasp rustled through the onlookers. It was a card that, to the untrained eye, seemed innocuous, but to those entwined in the hand, it was a potential game-changer, introducing the possibility of a flush for my opponent.

In that moment, amidst the scent of cigars and the gentle hum of conversation, my past and present collided. The tense uncertainty mirrored the unpredictable and oftentimes terrifying moments experienced in the deserts far from home.

Yet, the internal storm was met with an unexpected ally – the strategic calm honed at the very table I sat. The skills forged in the fire of countless hands and carefully navigated bluffs rose to the surface, steadying trembling hands and quelling the thundering in my chest.

The decision was made with a tactical tranquility, and I folded, retracting my hands from the battlefield and surrendering the amassed chips to my opponent, who, with a knowing nod, revealed the victorious flush his hand had concealed.

Losses, once a trigger, became lessons. Defeat at the poker table, while initially a sting, transformed into a catalyst for growth, reflection, and adaptation. Unlike the battles fought in uniform, losses here were devoid of the devastating, irreversible consequences that haunted my nightmares.

This safe, structured environment to experience loss, to navigate chaos, provided not only a diversion but also a gentle, unspoken therapy. Every folded hand was a practice in letting go, in strategic retreat, and in choosing battles - not out of fear or trigger but from a place of calm strategy and measured risk.

In poker, I discovered a pathway to reshape my relationship with loss, chaos, and unpredictability. Each shuffle of the cards, while bringing forth the ghosts of chaos, also brought opportunities to engage, to understand, and to navigate through it, gradually healing wounds that had long lay hidden beneath the surface.

Closing the cards and stacking the chips, I, Shaun, found myself gazing into the gentle chaos of the poker table, seeing not just a game but a metaphor for life itself.

In the shuffle of the deck, I found the unpredictable journey of life, the dealing of hands revealing that some battles are chosen for us, while others we bravely select ourselves. Each player at the table carried their strategy, their personality, and yet, we were all bound by the same uncertainty, the same fold or play that life often thrusts upon us.

In the hands I was dealt, I found reflections of moments from the battlefields of Afghanistan to the internal struggles within. Each card laid before me was a testament that even in the seemingly perfect, and in the apparent assurance of Aces, vulnerability lingered, reminding that strength often resides not in the absence of weakness but in its acknowledgement, in the strategic folds as much as in the triumphant plays.

A favorite quote came to mind, whispering wisdom through the clinks of the chips and the soft shuffles of cards: *"You have to know how to accept rejection and reject acceptance."* - Ray Bradbury.

I learned that the strongest hands could lose and that the weakest could, with guile and strategy, steal the pot. My journey through the hands of poker, from the sandy dunes of Afghanistan to the secluded haven of a Myrtle Beach poker room, became a lesson in navigating life's unpredictable tides, finding peace within the chaos, and carving a pathway through healing amidst the shuffle of life's deck.

And so, I stepped forward, with cards in hand, ready to play the next round of life's unpredictable game, ever-steering through the nuanced dance of acceptance and rejection, of knowing when to hold on and when to let go.

With this metaphorical note, we close the chapter, finding quiet wisdom within the clamor of shuffled decks and strategic plays. My journey continues, exploring further pathways of healing, strategies for life, and the continued dance with the unpredictable hands we are dealt. We'll explore these moments together, revealing more chapters of a soldier finding peace amidst chaos, with a deck of cards in hand.

CHAPTER 3

THE RULES OF THE GAME: LEARNING POKER

The gentle hum of the poker room, the tactile feel of the chips, and the subtle tension between the players provided a symphony of focus that I instinctively leaned into. Here, amidst the underground room filled with camaraderie and the unspoken complexities of the game, a new challenge unfolded before me.

The Basics and Strategies of Poker

Learning poker felt like diving into a new language. It wasn't merely about grasping the basic rules, but about plunging into the layers of strategy, psychology, and the delicate art that enveloped the game.

At its core, poker is a dance of variance, skill, and strategy, where players wage chips on the might of their hand. The very objective is to amass chips - either by holding the best hand or persuading others of the same. The rankings, from High Card to Royal Flush, seamlessly integrated into my understanding. Still, the true allure lay beyond just the mechanics.

In this world, the term 'nuts' wasn't just about the best possible hand. It was a metaphor for those moments when holding the best could be misconstrued as pride. The 'bluff' wasn't just a tactic; it was a life lesson, teaching me that sometimes, showing strength amidst vulnerability is a strategy – relevant not just on the felt but in the daily battles of life.

Finding Focus and Mental Stimulation

The profound focus demanded by these strategies provided me an unexpected form of escapism. Each decision at the poker table necessitated undivided attention, precise calculations, and keen observations of opponents. The deeper I submerged myself into the intricacies and subtleties of poker strategy, the more I discovered a mental sanctuary that shielded me from the relentless, haunting memories of war.

I remember a particular evening, dimly lit ambiance, echoes of friendly chatter, with my fingers tracing the cold, familiar surface of the clay chips. In those moments, my mind found its sanctuary, an engagement so intricate yet detached from the visceral remnants of my past.

Every dealt hand was a puzzle awaiting my solution. Crunching odds, discerning player tendencies, making strategic calls – this mental gymnastics allowed my mind to anchor itself in the now, distancing itself from past triggers and focusing on a cognitive challenge.

Parallels Between Poker and Coping Strategies

As I began to unearth the symbiotic relationship between my mental wellbeing and poker, undeniable parallels started to surface, drawing lines between the strategies at play on the poker table and the tools that aided in managing my PTSD.

1.Emotional Control: Just as I mastered the art of a poker face, concealing intentions and emotions from adversaries, I also learned emotional regulation. I realized that mastering my reactions, both at the table and in life, handed me the reins to navigate through any storm.

2. Strategic Thinking: The adaptations and moves I made in poker mirrored my daily life, where I found being tactical in managing my triggers and setting up coping strategies to be paramount.

3. Risk Management: Deciding when to play a semi-bluff and when to fold was like evaluating risks in real-life situations. It taught me to weigh the pros and cons in various facets of my life, especially concerning my mental health.

4. Accepting Loss: Every poker player, myself included, confronts defeat. I honed the skill of handling losses at the

table, an ability that cascaded into accepting and navigating through the valleys in my healing journey.

5. Patience: In poker, as in healing, patience was paramount. Neither progress nor winning came in a straight line. It was the collective effect of countless small choices, coupled with the tenacity to remain patient through ups and downs, that culminated in triumph over time.

As I spent countless nights engrossed in the rhythm of shuffling cards and the weight of poker chips, I inadvertently crafted a haven where my restless mind found a form of reprieve. Here, the tenets of poker braided with my life lessons, birthing a unique narrative where strategy, recuperation, and a deck of cards melded into my tale of resilience.

And so, my story continued, with cards clutched close and many chips still to be wagered, venturing deeper into the interplay of recovery within strategic confines.

The draw to poker wasn't just about potential riches or the exhilarating risk with each bet for me. Instead, it morphed into an unexpected refuge, a place where my mind, scarred by the traumas of war, discovered a semblance of calm amidst the strategic intricacies the game demanded.

Basics and Strategies of Poker

Diving into poker meant immersing myself in a world rich in strategy, chance, and human dynamics. While the foundational rules appeared simple—each player gets a hand and decides to bet, call, or fold based on their card's strength against the community cards—the genuine depth of poker existed beyond its surface.

In Texas Hold'em, I'd be dealt two private cards (hole cards) that were mine alone. Then, five community cards were laid out face-up on the 'board'. Every player, including me, used these shared community cards with their hole cards to craft the best possible five-card poker hand. The pot went to the player with the top hand or the last one standing after others have bowed out.

The strength of a hand could be as basic as a High Card or scale up to the revered Royal Flush. Yet, the cards in my hand were merely a part of the challenge. The true essence of poker for me lay in making strategic bets, mastering the art of bluffing, and maintaining a sharp awareness of other players' patterns and potential moves. A formidable player, like I aspired to be, operated at the intersection of mathematical acumen, intuitive psychology, and a sprinkle of audacity.

Finding Focus and Mental Stimulation in Poker

For me, poker became a sanctuary of mental exertion that was oddly soothing. The need to remain perpetually sharp and deliberate with each move created a shield against my haunting memories from Afghanistan. In this space of cards and chips, my mind found a detour, moving away from the harrowing echoes of war and into a realm of strategy and numbers, providing not just a diversion but a unique form of cognitive therapy.

Instead of being haunted by gunfire, fear, and loss, I found moments of respite, focusing on calculating odds, discerning potential bluffs from opponents, and making strategic decisions. Every card dealt was an invitation to step further from the mental battlefield, diving deeper into a world where control, decision-making, and analytical prowess took center stage.

Drawing Parallels: Poker Strategies and My PTSD Coping Strategies

Interestingly, I started seeing parallels between the tactics I employed at the poker table and those that helped me cope with PTSD. The measured risks, the need to remain centered and focused during the game, and the skill of reading others while masking my own emotions—these nuances started aligning with my daily strategies for navigating my mental health challenges.

Just as in poker where one must know when to fold, recognizing that some battles aren't worth the risk, I learned the significance of picking my battles in life, understanding when to retreat from potentially triggering situations. The act of bluffing in poker mirrored times when

I'd put on a brave face for the world, despite the internal struggles. Deciphering players at the poker table transitioned into a heightened sensitivity in social situations, as I began reading non-verbal cues with a newfound acumen.

In its elaborate dance of strategy, risk, and emotional mastery, poker became a metaphorical compass for me, shedding light on handling life post-war, post-trauma. Amidst the shuffle of cards and the rhythmic clink of chips, I discovered an oasis of calm, an unexpected haven where my battle-worn mind found moments of peace.

"Life, much like poker, demands that we sometimes play the hand we're dealt, while at other times, we fold and await the next round. It's not solely about the cards but how we use them, how we traverse the bluffs, the gambles, and the unpredictable twists of the game. And occasionally, in the stillness of a folded hand, I unearthed profound strength and an unforeseen serenity."

With these sentiments, Chapter 3 seamlessly weaves into the broader narrative of my journey, where each card dealt is not just a possible win or loss but a step towards understanding, healing, and mastering the intricate dance of life and mind.

CHAPTER 4

EMOTIONAL EQUILIBRIUM: POKER FACE AND MINDFULNESS

Hawaiian Gardens Casino, California, with its lively yet inconspicuous charm, always fascinated me in a peculiar way. The moment I stepped through its doors, I, Shaun, was enveloped by the electric buzz of anticipation, excitement, and that sweet yet somehow tense melody of shuffled cards and chiming chips. This wasn't the semi-clandestine familiarity of that Myrtle Beach poker room; it was a new arena, a place where my skills would be tested by strangers who had no knowledge of my past or the battles I was fighting within.

It's curious, the first time I sat at a table there, my hands, ever so slightly, trembled. It wasn't fear, nor was it solely excitement. It was an awareness of stepping into an environment where the stakes were different, where the table was sprinkled with professionals who played not just for fun or camaraderie, but for their livelihoods.

One memorable evening, I found myself seated across from a seasoned pro. His eyes, steady and unyielding, betrayed no emotion as he smoothly slid a stack of chips into the pot. The cards in my hand were decent, but it was his unwavering demeanor that planted a seed of doubt in my mind. There was a lesson to be learned here - one that extended beyond the confines of the poker table.

Maintaining a "poker face", it's an art and a skill, an enigma that one needs to crack in order to be victorious in this cerebral game. It's not just about not showing fear, joy, or disappointment, but also about exhibiting control, mastery over one's own emotions and thoughts. I realized that this stoic, unyielding expression was akin to mindfulness - a practice of being present, of holding oneself in a balanced space where emotions neither leak nor erupt but exist in a harmonious equilibrium.

My military training had always stressed the importance of control under pressure, yet PTSD had shaken that foundation to its core, causing eruptions of memories and emotions in the least expected moments. Here, however, amidst the cool and collected players at Hawaiian Gardens, the concept took a new form. The poker face became both a shield and a mirror, reflecting my own internal struggles and triumphs amidst the concealed emotions.

And unexpectedly, poker turned into a silent teacher of mindfulness. As my mind oscillated between the cards in hand and the memories of a tumultuous past, I found an unspoken resonance in maintaining that emotional equilibrium. The ability to hold a steady gaze while internally calculating odds, observing opponents, and making strategic decisions, turned into a metaphor for dealing with daily triggers and stressors. My ability to mask my emotions at the poker table began translating into an ability to observe, acknowledge, and manage them off of it.

In moments where a sudden flashback threatened to overtake me or a trigger loomed large in the horizon, the learned steadiness, the emotional grounding I practiced at the poker table, started becoming a tool, a mechanism that gradually enabled me to regain control over the tumultuous waves of unexpected emotion.

My journey in Hawaiian Gardens was not merely one of mastering a game, it became a pathway through which I navigated the tempestuous seas of my own psychological battles. I learned that the best players aren't just masters of the game, but masters of themselves, able to navigate through an ocean of unpredictability with a serene, undisturbed facade. This understanding didn't just make me a better player; it made me better equipped to face the everyday challenges that lay outside the realm of dealt cards and wagered chips.

Navigating through these experiences, poker became less of a game and more of a silent companion, whispering lessons of patience, control, and mindful presence amidst the chaotic spirals that sometimes sought to engulf me.

"Luck is what happens when preparation meets opportunity." - Seneca, Roman Philosopher

This quote subtly ties into the theme of preparation and emotional regulation, where the "preparation" can be likened to the mastery of one's own emotions and mental state - a pivotal element both in poker and everyday life. The "opportunity" reflects those moments where emotional equilibrium is tested, whether on the poker table facing a potential high-stakes loss or in daily life encountering an unexpected trigger. In these intersections, our "luck" or outcome is influenced by how well our internal preparation - our mental and emotional balance - allows us to navigate through them.

CHAPTER 5

CALCULATED RISKS: DECISION MAKING AND ACCOUNTABILITY

It's strange, but sitting there, amid the hum of whispers and the rhythmic clinking of chips, I found a sort of sanctuary at the poker table. A place where the chaos of my mind seemed to pause, allowing me to fully immerse myself into the game. It was during these moments, while I, Shaun, tried to decipher my opponents' strategies and calculate the risks of each move, that I learned something invaluable about decision-making and accountability, not just in poker but in life as well.

The essence of poker isn't merely in the cards dealt to you but in the decisions, you make with them. There's always a moment of hesitation, a brief pause in time where you weigh the odds, scrutinize your opponents, and then make a choice. To fold or to play, to risk or to secure, each decision comes with its own bundle of what-ifs and potential consequences.

I remember one night at the Hawaiian Gardens Casino, where I was in a seemingly favorable position. The stakes were high, and my hand was promising - a pair of Kings. My pulse thrummed in my ears as I pushed a hefty pile of chips into the center, an aggressive bet signaling confidence. My opponents, seasoned players with years of experience etched into their poker faces, didn't waiver. They mirrored my bet without hesitation.

As the cards on the board were revealed, my confidence wavered but I pushed through, maintaining my poker face. It came down to the river, the final card, and my heart sank as it did nothing to improve my hand. Yet, there was something in me that refused to back down. I made the final bet, pushing all my chips into the anxious circle of anticipation in the center.

And then, like a swift pull of the rug beneath my feet, my confidence shattered as my opponent revealed a pair of Aces. A superior hand that toppled my Kings and with it, my hefty pile of chips slid away from me.

It was a moment of bitter defeat, yet amid the sting of loss, a seed of understanding took root. Every decision I made at that table, from the confident bets to the final reluctant push of my chips, was mine and mine alone. The accountability of my choices was crystal clear, as tangible as the empty space in front of me, once occupied by my chips. It was a costly lesson, yet invaluable in its teaching. I learned that decisions must be calculated, detached from ego and emotion, and deeply rooted in the reality of the situation - not the reality as we wish it to be.

My experiences on the battlefield taught me the harsh reality of life and death decisions, but poker, in its own unique way, taught me about calculated risks and accountability in a space where the stakes were significant yet non-lethal. It taught me to separate hope from reality, to make decisions based on what *is* rather than what I *hoped* would be.

This understanding became a cornerstone in managing my life and my PTSD. I learned to evaluate situations more pragmatically, to weigh my options and anticipate potential outcomes, and most importantly, to be prepared to accept and deal with the consequences of my choices, whether they be losses or victories.

Poker, with its blend of skill, strategy, and an ever-present element of chance, became a metaphor for my life journey. It reminded me that while I cannot control every aspect of life, I can control my responses, my decisions, and subsequently take accountability for the paths those decisions lead me down.

Gleaming lights, incessant chatters, and the unmissable allure of chance - Las Vegas, a city where fortunes are made and lost on the turn of a card. My heart brimmed with anticipation and a pinch of anxiety as I stepped into the opulent poker room at the Bellagio, a place renowned for its high-stake games and the legends who graced its tables. This was my first attempt at the 5-10 stakes, a step up from what I had grown accustomed to. My pulse quickened as I sat down, feeling the weight of the challenge before me.

Earlier that evening, something serendipitous had happened. I had crossed paths with the poker legend himself, Doyle Brunson, right in front of Bobby's Room, named after Bobby Baldwin, and renowned for hosting some of the highest-stakes poker games in the world. The excitement was palpable as I respectfully asked for a photograph, a memento of meeting the Godfather of Poker. Doyle, with his timeless charm and kindness, obliged.

With the thrill of that encounter still simmering within me, I found myself amidst a hand that was, under normal circumstances, an easy fold. A 10-2, offsuit - objectively a terrible starting hand, but famously known as the "Doyle Brunson" owing to the legend winning the WSOP Main Event twice with it. A hand that, after meeting the man himself, I felt compelled to play.

The table was tense, a pot that had bloated far beyond what one would expect with the cards in my hand. I could sense the skepticism from my opponents, perhaps attributing my play to the recklessness of a novice. Little did they know, this was a small tribute to a chance meeting with a legend.

The flop came down, astonishingly favorable: 10-10-2. A full house. My heart skipped a beat, yet my face remained an impenetrable mask of calmness. The turn and the river were inconsequential. I kept my bets strategic and enticing, ensuring that my opponents remained hooked, yet oblivious to the strength of my hand.

The moment of revelation, the showdown, was met with gasps and grumbles from around the table, particularly from one player, whose significantly superior starting hand had been toppled by my seemingly irrational play. His stack slid towards me, his eyes ablaze with a mixture of disbelief and indignation. Yet, in his gaze, I saw a reluctant glimmer of acknowledgment - the understanding that sometimes, against all odds and logic, the underdog can prevail.

As I raked in the chips, the symbolism of the moment was not lost on me. Yes, sometimes in life, impractical decisions, guided by intuition or emotion, do pay off, writing stories that defy logic and statistics. However, I realized that it's crucial to acknowledge such instances for what they are - outliers, rather than the norm.

The crux lay in the harmony between calculated risks, like those refined through countless hands of poker, and the occasional leap of faith, driven by a moment of inspiration or a surge of emotion. The balance between these two aspects of decision-making is where I found my stride, both at the poker table and in managing the labyrinthine complexities of life and PTSD.

In closing the chapter, the words of the revered scientist, Albert Einstein, resonate deeply: "A ship is always safe at shore, but that is not what it's built for." The anecdote from the tables at Bellagio isn't merely a tale of triumph amidst the revered walls where countless legends have gambled their fortunes away; it's emblematic of a journey where risks, both calculated and whimsical, chart the path ahead.

Playing the 10-2, contrary to established strategy, and sailing into the stormy waters of high-stakes poker was a risk – one that paid off spectacularly in the moment, but warranted reflection upon the sustainability of such tactics. The safety of adhering strictly to odds and probabilities in poker, and similarly, maintaining predictable routines in life, offers its own semblance of security. However, it's often in the undulating waves of risks and challenges where we unearth our true potential, learning to navigate through uncertainty with sagacity and a touch of daring.

This serves not only as a testament to the spirited endeavors at the poker table but also as a metaphor for life, especially when combatting the tempestuous seas of an ordeal like PTSD. We can employ learned strategies for stability and predictability but embracing calculated risks is pivotal to truly live, grow, and perhaps, win, both at the table and in the grander scheme of life.

CHAPTER 6

THE POWER OF COMMUNITY: SOCIAL INTERACTION AND SUPPORT

Lingering in the dimly lit corners of underground poker rooms and elegantly adorned casino floors, I, Shaun, found an unexpected treasure trove of camaraderie and emotional sustenance within the poker community. The clinks of chips and the subtle, yet exuberant, rustle of shuffled cards became a symphony that heralded not just a game, but a sanctuary where I discovered belonging and understanding.

To an outsider, poker might be perceived as a stark battlefield, where individuals engage in a silent psychological war, shrouded by their impassive poker faces. However, beneath the apparent stoicism lies a community, abundant with empathetic bonds forged between its members. Engaging with different personas at the table, ranging from the sagacious old-timers with stories aplenty, to the young, fervent dreamers, hungry for their big break, I found an eclectic, yet harmoniously bound tapestry of connections.

One of my most cherished memories embarks from a modest poker room, fragrant with the aroma of rich mahogany and subdued excitement. As I settled into a seat, enveloped by the familiar and comforting cacophony of poker room sounds, an elderly gentleman to my right offered a warm, genuine smile. His eyes gleamed, revealing unspoken stories of life, both on and off the felt.

"Name's Charlie," he spoke, his voice laced with a gentle, soothing cadence. And thus, we embarked upon a journey of shared tales, laden with laughter, empathy, and unspoken understanding. In Charlie, I found not just an opponent on the felt, but a comrade in life. He shared tales of yesteryears, of games played in hidden backrooms, and of friendships forged amidst the highs and lows of poker hands.

The poker table became an arena where the shroud of my struggles with PTSD was acknowledged, yet not judged. It was a place where my struggles were neither downplayed nor amplified. The community provided a balance, helping me perceive my experiences as just one facet of my being, rather than an all-encompassing identity.

Over the tables, across the numerous hands dealt, camaraderie flourished amidst heartfelt conversations and shared silences. My fellow players, many of whom harbored their own burdens and triumphs, inadvertently fostered a space where I could exist unfettered by the crippling labels or stigmas that often silently tail mental health struggles.

In the poker community, I found an unspoken, yet profound, support network, where moments of vulnerability were met with either comforting gestures or respectful distances, offering a solace that was both liberating and empowering. Amidst the calculated bluffs, folds, and calls, there transpired a silent acknowledgment of our shared humanity - our victories, our losses, our strengths, and our frailties.

Navigating through the multifaceted world of poker, I found not only a stimulating mental challenge but also a space where the invisible walls erected by PTSD seemed to crumble, revealing pathways toward connection, understanding, and genuine companionship. While the chips danced and cards flew, friendships solidified, becoming a grounding force that provided stability amidst the chaotic tempest of internal struggles.

It was here, amidst the seemingly inconspicuous interactions and shared glances, that I discovered the undeniable power of community within the realms of poker rooms and tournament floors. The unanticipated journey through poker's social labyrinth subtly, yet profoundly, contributed to the armamentarium that empowered me to navigate through the convoluted terrains of PTSD.

May 29th, 2018, marked a pivotal juncture in my journey - both in poker and my inner emotional pilgrimage. As I, Shaun, strolled through the bustling, spirited halls of the

Rio, enveloped by the jubilant echoes of the World Series of Poker (WSOP), an electrifying surge of anticipation permeated through every fiber of my being. With a hopeful heart, I registered for a $200 daily afternoon tournament, my pulse dancing in tandem with the shuffle of decks across countless tables.

Seated amidst a myriad of faces, each mask harboring tales of dreams, triumphs, and adversities, I navigated through the sea of cards and chips with an unbridled spirit, my demeanor radiating an infectious positivity. Every fold, call, and raise transcended beyond mere gameplay, morphing into a silent conversation, where my soul, unshackled from the chains of despair, basked in a liberating light of genuine connections.

As hands progressed and players conceded to the unforgiving whims of chance and skill, a peculiarly warm camaraderie blossomed amidst the competitive battleground. Every exchanged smile, shared chuckle, and consoling pat on the back wove into a tapestry of unspoken solidarity, where each of us, despite our individual pursuits of victory, found solace and kinship in our shared love for the game.

My journey through the tournament, punctuated by the harmonious clinks of escalating chip stacks and the empathetic glances shared during moments of defeat, culminated in a fifth-place finish. Yet, the joy derived from that accomplishment paled in comparison to the overwhelming emotional clarity and affection that enveloped me.

As I basked in the ephemeral, yet profound, glory of the moment, three familiar faces from the earlier stages of the tournament emerged from the crowd. Their eyes sparkled with genuine joy and respect, and amidst the cacophonous cheers and subtle nods of acknowledgment, an unspoken bond was forged. These individuals, who had witnessed the ebb and flow of my journey through each hand, had lingered, silently championing my journey amidst their own.

We convened, not as mere acquaintances forged through a game but as friends bound by shared experiences, to a cozy burger joint, where the aroma of grilled delights intermingled with our tales of triumphs and defeats, both on and off the felt. Our laughter echoed through the space, as we, liberated from our intrinsic battles, basked in a moment suspended in time, where friendships blossomed amidst shared vulnerabilities and victories.

In those moments, amidst the playful banter and shared reflections, I recognized the power of community, of unpretentious, supportive relationships, in crafting a haven where emotional burdens were acknowledged, shared, and subtly alleviated. The poker table, beyond a mere platform for a beloved card game, had morphed into a sanctuary where emotional walls crumbled, revealing the authentic, unguarded spirit beneath.

The friendships forged amidst the competitive flames and shared silences of the poker table became pillars of strength, providing not only a supportive foundation during times of internal tumult but also shaping a conduit through which I discovered mechanisms to navigate the complexities of PTSD.

"Life, like poker has an element of risk. It shouldn't be avoided. It should be faced."
– Edward Norton in "Rounders"

This quote, from one of the most iconic poker films, subtly intertwines the essence of poker with the profoundness of life's journey, encapsulating the beautiful synergy between facing life's uncertainties and embracing every hand dealt to us in poker, and perhaps, in friendships as well. The associations, emotions, and bonds formed at the poker table mirror life's intricate web of connections, underscoring the unspoken, yet deeply felt kinship amongst players who share not just a game, but life's multifaceted journey together.

CHAPTER 7

HEALING THROUGH CHALLENGE: MENTAL AGILITY AND RESILIENCE

With every card dealt, poker unfurls a myriad of possibilities, a maze of potential outcomes, and choices to navigate. My days spent pondering over poker tables, dissecting hands, and developing strategies were not just pastime activities. These experiences were a continuous, unscripted workshop, enhancing my cognitive abilities, from honing concentration to deciphering patterns and strategically planning every move.

I recall vividly, the complexities of each hand, each game, demanding my utmost attention, my mind toggling between present actions and predicting potential future moves. It became a cognitive exercise, each game sharpening my mind, aiding me in developing a mental agility I hadn't realized I was capable of. My thoughts were no longer sluggish or stunted by the haunting shadows of my past. They were lively, energized, and stimulated by the complex, strategic gameplay before me.

Anchored in the rich mental stimulation that poker provided, was a subtle, yet powerful foundation for developing resilience. The game inherently posed constant challenges, situations that demanded careful consideration, and rapid, adept decision-making. There were moments of triumph and instances of defeat, yet each hand dealt, whether victorious or not, beckoned me to persevere, to continue, to keep playing.

In the intricate web of poker's challenges, I found parallels to life's battles, the ups, and downs, the wins and losses, each demanding a choice: to relent or to forge ahead. The game, in its essence, mirrored life's tumultuous journey, cultivating within me a resilience, a mental fortitude to confront, comprehend, and conquer the challenges that lay ahead.

The insurmountable became surmountable. The inescapable shadows of PTSD, which once enveloped my very being, began to retreat, overpowered by the burgeoning light of mental and emotional resilience. As I embraced each challenge on the poker table, it inadvertently became a symbolic act of facing and overcoming my personal, inner turmoil.

I remember a specific instance when I was deep into a tournament, the stakes were high, and I was placed in a precarious position, one that required astute strategic thinking and an unwavering emotional steadiness. My hands carefully concealed my hole cards, the Ace of Hearts and the Nine of Spades - a strong starting hand but by no means a guarantee of victory. As the community cards were revealed, a flutter of anxiety and excitement danced within me, yet my expression remained an unyielding mask of calm.

In that moment, every ounce of my being was absorbed into the game, my thoughts crystalline, free from the haunting specters of war. Each decision, each calculated risk taken on the poker table was a step towards reclaiming a piece of myself that was lost amidst the rubble and chaos of the battlefield. My mind, once entrapped within the harrowing memories of war, was now liberated, engrossed in a game that offered not only an escape but a path towards healing, towards mental resilience.

Poker, in its multifaceted complexity, became a conduit through which I was able to channel the tumultuous energy of my experiences, transforming them into a constructive, cognitive, and emotional outlet. It wasn't merely a game; it was a silent ally, facilitating a quiet yet profound healing through every challenge faced, every hand played, and every risk calculated.

The enchanting world of poker, with its potent blend of challenge, risk, and strategic thinking, became an unexpected yet welcome companion on my journey towards healing and mental and emotional resilience.

My eyes flickered briefly towards my opponent, trying to glean any semblance of his strategy from his demeanor. But he, like me, had perfected the art of the poker face - an unwavering, unreadable facade. I pondered deeply on the potential paths this hand could traverse, the probabilities and possibilities cascading through my mind like a vibrant kaleidoscope of strategic avenues.

As the community cards unfolded before us – a King of Diamonds, a Ten of Hearts, and a Jack of Spades on the flop, followed by an inconspicuous Two of Clubs on the turn – my pulse quickened. The board was teasing an enticing straight draw, should a queen decide to grace us on the river. I pondered, was he, too, awaiting the arrival of the coveted queen?

I found myself at a crucial juncture, where calculated risk brushed shoulders with hopeful aspiration. The sizeable pot, burgeoning with the amassed chips, whispered temptingly. My mind fluttered back to the days where decisions were a matter of life and death, a stark contrast to the friendly competition before me, yet somehow, in this context, it felt similarly significant.

Was it just a game? Certainly. But it was also a metaphorical arena where I learned to dance with uncertainty, to gracefully navigate the choppy waters of chance and risk. And so, I called, advancing forward into the unknown with a cautious optimism.

The river unveiled a Queen of Clubs. My heart swelled with a quiet, understated victory as my straight materialized, yet my countenance betrayed nothing of the triumph that swirled within. Opponents pushed their chips forward, none the wiser of the serendipity that had unfolded before me.

I made my bet, a sea of chips cascading forward with an assured ease. The final calls were made, and as the cards were revealed, a sense of accomplishment enfolded me. Not just for the victorious hand, but for the realization that the game, in its myriad of ups and downs, of risks and rewards, had sculpted my mind into something resilient, adaptable, and unabashedly hopeful.

It was more than a game; it was a subtle reminder that even amidst the uncertainty, the unexpected triumphs were possible. That even in the throes of chaos, there exists the potential for unanticipated victories and lessons to be unearthed. This, I found, was the true essence of poker, a medium through which I learned to embrace challenges with a composed mind and to observe the unfolding of life with a perceptive, strategic eye.

In each card dealt, I discovered not just a game, but a metaphor for life, teaching me the power of mental agility, of nurturing a resilient spirit capable of facing the unforeseen challenges with a gentle, yet unwavering strength.

"Resilience is not a simple, single virtue, but a sort of mental and emotional martial art. It's a series of maneuvers and methods used to overcome, circumvent, adapt to, or make the best of significant adversity." – Chris Kresser

This quote beautifully wraps up our chapter by emphasizing that resilience isn't merely an intrinsic quality but a crafted skill, honed and refined through confronting and navigating adversities, much like the strategic depth and mental agility required at the poker table. When we apply this mindset to life's challenges, we forge a path of resilience, persistently evolving and adapting to the various hurdles placed before us.

CHAPTER 8

UNIVERSALITY OF POKER: HOW IT CAN HELP OTHERS

Ever since my fortuitous tumble into the realm of poker, I, Shaun, have found myself marveling at the inexplicably transformative power of the game. It was never just about the cards, the chips, or the pot, but about the camaraderie, the mental engagement, and perhaps, most potently, the escape it provided from the clutches of my tormenting recollections.

The poker table became a sanctuary, where people from all walks of life gathered, each harboring their own tales of joy, sorrow, victory, and defeat. I met individuals like Tom, a firefighter who sought refuge in the cards and chips from the traumatically vivid memories of perishing souls he couldn't save. There was Lisa, a nurse, who found that the calculated risks of poker provided a welcome contrast to the life-and-death decisions she navigated during her excruciating shifts at the hospital.

It gradually became clear that poker offered more than just a fleeting escape; it became a universally applicable balm, soothing the emotional and mental afflictions that spanned various professions, experiences, and traumas.

It wasn't merely the game; it was the collective solidarity that enveloped us in that room, shielding us from our personal tempests, if only for a moment. The inclusive nature of poker, where anyone from a seasoned professional to an absolute novice could sit shoulder to shoulder, sharing in the same blend of exhilaration and vulnerability, brought forth a unique therapeutic environment.

I wondered, could this 'poker therapy' be something more structured, something intentionally woven into treatment for PTSD and other mental health struggles?

Mulling over this thought, my mind wandered to countless veterans, like me, who navigated the tumultuous seas of reintegration and the myriad of struggles it presented. Similarly, first responders, healthcare professionals, and others embedded in high-stress environments were entwined in a perpetual battle against their mental demons.

The emotional fortitude and mental agility honed at the poker table were not merely applicable to me, but potentially universal in their utility. It was about learning when to hold firm and when to fold, understanding that some battles, no matter how fervently fought, would not culminate in victory. It was about recognizing that vulnerability did not equate to weakness and that seeking support was both a strength and a strategy for survival.

The more I dwelled on the universality of poker, the more stories surfaced of individuals harnessing its therapeutic potential in their own lives. Conversations, news articles, and anecdotes amalgamated, providing a compelling narrative that poker was more than a game – it was a vessel of healing, not just for a solitary individual, but for a collective.

As I reflect on these stories and my own journey, I envision a future where the transformative power of poker is acknowledged and harnessed to its fullest, assisting others as it has assisted me, providing solace, community, and a treasured respite from the tumultuous storms that rage within.

As the World Series of Poker (WSOP) unfolded in the bustling and effervescent environment of Las Vegas in 2022, I, Shaun, found myself seated at a table, surrounded by a motley crew of players, each engrossed in the riveting Salute to Warriors tournament. Amidst the clinking of chips and the subtle, yet distinctive rustle of shuffled cards, my gaze was inadvertently drawn to a gentleman seated directly across from me, in seat one - Paul.

Paul, with his genial demeanor and contemplative eyes, emanated a certain calmness that belied the turbulent waves of experiences lurking beneath his serene exterior. With every hand dealt, I observed how his fingers, steadfast and gentle, gracefully maneuvered the cards, revealing glimpses of a man who was no stranger to navigating through tumultuous terrains.

Intrigued and instinctively drawn towards his story, during one of the breaks, I sauntered over, and we engaged in what began as a casual conversation about hands played and strategies employed. The barriers, however, began to crumble, revealing deeper, more poignant tales interwoven with trauma, healing, and the unanticipated solace found within the confines of poker.

Paul, an ER doctor, shared tales of nights steeped in the harrowing cries of pain, the palpable grip of despair, and the desperate battle against the ever-ticking clock, striving to pull souls back from the precipice of the abyss. His eyes, reflective pools of countless stories, spoke of the unbearable weight of lives lost, and the immense pressure that veiled his every waking moment in the emergency room.

He shared, "Poker, in its enigmatic ways, became an unexpected sanctuary. A place where decisions, while holding weight, were not enshrouded with the oppressive burden of life and death."

The poker table became his arena where he could exercise control without the engulfing shadow of irreversible consequences. The camaraderie he found within the poker community, a beautiful tapestry of varied souls, provided a comforting embrace, a place where judgments were suspended, and understanding was generously extended.

As he spoke, his words seemed to dance, intertwining with my own experiences, revealing the universality of our journeys. Both of us, from vastly different worlds, found a semblance of peace, a respite, within the confines of this game. Paul found a way to unburden himself from the overpowering weight of his profession, to seek a momentary escape where his decisions were his own, liberated from the pervasive life-or-death reality that permeated his every day and night in the ER.

I listened, absorbing every word, recognizing the parallel threads that bound our stories, marveling at the therapeutic universality of poker. How it offered a unique form of reprieve for souls like Paul and me, providing a space where we could lay down our burdens, if only for a moment, amidst the shuffling of cards and the subtle rhythms of chip stacks being meticulously counted and recounted.

As we re-entered the playing arena, resuming our positions amidst the gentle hum of ongoing conversations and the resonating sounds emblematic of poker, I realized that our stories were merely two amongst countless others, waiting to be heard, acknowledged, and understood.

In this diverse community of players, from all walks of life, the poker table was not merely a physical space; it was a shared experience, a collective journey towards healing, understanding, and an unspoken, yet deeply felt, camaraderie.

Paul, with his gracious smile and weathered eyes, became not just an opponent but a kindred spirit, a reminder of the power of shared experiences, empathy, and the quietly potent healing embedded within the world of poker.

Amidst the vibrant atmosphere of the 2022 WSOP, within the heart of the bustling casino and under the bright, dazzling lights, the "Employees Only" event unfolded, creating a distinctive bubble within which an unexpected tale of resilience blossomed. At the final table, an intriguing blend of anticipation, excitement, and camaraderie permeated the air, transcending beyond the mere mechanics of the game into something deeper, something profoundly human.

I, Shaun, was enrapt by the intermingling tales that breathed life into our game, offering glimpses into the worlds that lay concealed behind each player's carefully maintained poker face. Here, amidst the shuffling cards and varying stacks of chips, the story of Rachel, a woman of unwavering strength and vibrant spirit, gracefully unfurled.

As we stepped away from the table for our final dinner break, our bodies eagerly soaking in the brief respite, our conversation naturally flowed into realms beyond poker. Rachel, with her eyes sparkling with a blend of fire and gentle warmth, began to share a chapter of her life that painted her journey within the casino walls.

She began, "Working in this casino, in this realm dominated largely by men, particularly as a woman, has been...an adventure, to say it lightly." Her laughter, light yet laced with underlying echoes of endured challenges, rippled through the air. "Poker became an unexpected ally, a space where I could assert control, enact decisions, and truly own my place."

Rachel's experiences as a woman navigating through the tumultuous waters of a casino environment, one often colored with bouts of inebriation and the unchecked liberties taken by patrons, presented a daily gauntlet of trials. A space where her strength was constantly tested by the abrasive winds of verbal abuses and unsolicited advances.

Yet, within the realm of poker, she found an unexpected sanctuary. A space where her decisions, strategy, and skills spoke louder than the unwarranted judgments and caustic words that were often hurled her way outside the poker arena.

She continued, "Poker allowed me a voice, a stance, and an empowerment that was often stripped away in the daily dealings with patrons. On this felt, I wasn't merely an object of unwarranted affections or a recipient of thoughtless jibes. I was a player, an equal, a strategist navigating through the waves of the game."

In poker, Rachel discovered a realm where her identity was not bound by her gender or the connotations thrust upon her by societal lenses. She was a player, skilled and respected for her gameplay, undeterred by the harsh echoes of the casino floor.

Her story resonated, intertwining with the threads of varied experiences at our table. Within her words lay the universal resonance of poker's unexpected healing - a space that offered not only an escape but also a reclaiming of power, control, and respect that was often denied in other domains of life.

As we reconnected with the rhythm of the game, Rachel's story lingered, an emblem of the unexpected paths towards healing and empowerment that poker offered to souls from all walks of life. Her journey, a testament to the silent yet potent resilience that permeated through the poker community, added a new layer to the rich tapestry that collectively wove us all together.

In these narratives, these deeply personal and varied journeys, the universality of poker as a source of solace, empowerment, and unexpected healing shone brightly, binding us all in silent, shared understanding and unspoken kinship. It subtly whispered of the potential that lay within the game, to traverse beyond mere recreation into realms of therapeutic and empowering experiences.

The stories etched into the felt of poker tables across the world are as varied and diverse as the individuals who bring them to life. From the spirited echoes of joyous victories to the solemn hush of a loss barely evaded, these narratives weave a colorful tapestry that illustrates the profound and multi-faceted impact of poker on the lives of countless individuals.

In my, Shaun's, journey, poker transformed from a mere game into a silent ally, a space where the tumultuous storms of past traumas were momentarily quelled, allowing for fleeting yet deeply cherished moments of tranquility and focus. Similarly, as seen in the stories of Paul and Rachel, the game morphed into an unexpected source of solace, empowerment, and resilience amidst the varying challenges that life unfurled.

It becomes compellingly clear that the nuances and strategies embedded within the game of poker offer a unique, universally accessible platform that intertwines mental stimulation, emotional regulation, and social connection into a potent blend with the potential to provide therapeutic benefits. But can these personal stories, these individual instances of healing and empowerment found within the confines of poker, be expanded into a wider, more structured form of therapeutic intervention?

Imagine a space where the strategies, decision-making skills, and emotional regulation required at the poker table are utilized as a structured form of therapy for individuals grappling with PTSD, anxiety, depression, or other mental health challenges. A space where the game acts as a conduit through which individuals can navigate through their struggles, find moments of respite, and perhaps, weave their path towards healing and recovery.

The potential application of poker as a form of therapy extends beyond the individual narratives and can potentially be molded into a structured intervention that encompasses the diverse therapeutic elements embedded within the game. The mental engagement, strategic thinking, emotional control, and social interaction that are intrinsic to poker, may, in a structured and supportive environment, provide a platform that facilitates cognitive engagement, emotional regulation, and social connectivity.

In a world where the pursuit of mental well-being is as varied and diverse as the individuals who embark upon it, the exploration into alternative, non-traditional forms of therapy, such as poker, presents an intriguing pathway. It's an avenue that intertwines recreation, mental stimulation, and emotional regulation into a seamless blend, offering an accessible and universal form of potential therapeutic intervention.

The exploration of poker, not merely as a game but as a potential therapeutic tool, opens up avenues for further research, exploration, and perhaps, the development of a novel approach towards mental health intervention that is universally accessible and can be tailored to cater to the unique needs of diverse individuals.

As we continue this exploration, we weave the tapestry with threads of countless stories, embodying the resilience, empowerment, and unexpected journeys towards healing found within the world of poker, expanding its reach beyond mere recreation into realms that softly whisper of potential, healing, and unexpected kinship.

"Here's to the invisible battles we fight, to the strength that is witnessed by none and to the hope that keeps us moving forward, step by unseen step. The silent wars within us often manifest the loudest victories." - Shaun, the unspoken warrior.

In essence, this quote embodies the silent, internal struggles faced by individuals grappling with PTSD and other mental health challenges. It is a nod of acknowledgment to the unseen battles, the quiet strength, and the resilient spirit that propels forward motion, even amidst the throes of challenge and despair. The nuanced healing, empowerment, and community found within the game of poker provides a subtle yet potent testament to these silent victories, crafting a narrative that resonates with resilience, silent strength, and the unwavering spirit of the warrior within.

CHAPTER 9

PLAYING IT FORWARD: ADVOCACY AND AWARENESS

Stepping into the world of advocacy, I've discovered, isn't simply about fighting for a cause. It's about being a voice for a silent struggle, a guide toward unseen pathways of healing, and a light illuminating the shadows where despair often hides. My journey with poker, unexpectedly filled with lessons, solace, and a community that became a haven, had grown into something far larger than the sum of its parts. It wasn't just my refuge; it was a wellspring of potential for others to tap into, a medium through which I wanted others to also find their peace and forge their resilience.

I remember distinctly, my first initiative to introduce poker as a therapeutic tool didn't occur in some grand hall or a well-organized conference. It was in a cozy little room, filled with a handful of veterans, a couple of decks of cards, and a palpable aura of camaraderie. The goal was simple - to extend the olive branch of healing that I found through poker, sharing not just a game, but a journey of recuperation and self-discovery.

My advocacy efforts have been shaped with an intentionality that stems from personal experience, driving a mission to promote poker as a means of therapy and mental rejuvenation. It's about maneuvering through the world of mental health with an unconventional method, one that merges strategic thinking, emotional control, and the development of a supportive community, weaving a network of healing that's subtly embedded in every shuffled deck, every bet, and every shared story around the poker table.

Looking toward the future, my vision envelops not only veterans like myself but anyone shackled by their own mental battles. The universality of poker lends itself to be a channel through which numerous individuals, from varied walks of life, can find a semblance of peace and a community that understands the unspoken struggles etched in their beings.

In my ongoing efforts, partnerships with veteran organizations and mental health advocates have become an integral pillar, ensuring that the message reaches far and wide, and the olive branch of poker therapy is extended to every hidden corner where someone might be silently struggling. Nurturing these alliances isn't just about widening the reach but deepening the impact, creating spaces where the healing power of poker is not just heard about but felt, experienced, and proliferated.

In essence, the advocacy for poker transcends beyond its strategic and entertaining attributes; it beckons toward a realm where mindfulness meets gameplay, where strategy intertwines with serenity, and where every table becomes a safe space, inviting individuals to lay down their guards, along with their cards, and embrace a journey where healing is dealt with in every hand played forward.

As we delve deeper into the realms of advocacy and awareness, the myriad stories, experiences, and unspoken bonds forged over numerous games of poker become the flag bearers of a silent revolution, one that whispers hope, strength, and resilience into the ears of those quietly battling their own wars within. My journey, interwoven with tales of both despair and victory, now seeks to become a beacon for others, lighting a path toward healing, one hand of poker at a time.

Steven sat, his posture slightly stooped yet eyes gleaming with a cautious optimism, across the poker table at one of our small events tailored specifically for veterans. His hands, mildly trembling, revealed not nerves about the game, but a deeper, more intimate battle that was always at play within him. His presence there, in a dimly lit room emanating with gentle murmurs and the shuffling of cards, was not just about poker. It was about salvation.

The first time I met Steven, he shared with me, with a voice barely above a whisper, that he was a 100% disabled Army veteran. The wars he fought transcended beyond the battlefield into his everyday existence, every waking moment becoming a silent struggle against the ghosts that relentlessly haunted him. His trauma was invisible to the naked eye, yet as tangible as the cards he held cautiously in his hands.

As we played, Steven, who initially shielded himself with a carefully crafted armor of solitude, gradually began to lower his guard. His eyes, once shrouded with an impenetrable veneer of stoicism, slowly warmed as he became engrossed in the game and the subtle camaraderie it fostered. The poker table became a sanctuary where judgments were suspended, and silent understandings were forged. It was a place where he could lay down his burdens alongside his bets, and every fold wasn't a surrender but a testament to vulnerability and trust.

One particular evening, after a casual game, Steven approached me, his eyes welling with an emotion that spoke volumes of gratitude and release. He shared that the friendships he had found across the poker table had become his lifeline, a balm to the gnawing solitude that often threatened to engulf him. The community around the poker table had unknowingly tethered him to a world he had felt estranged from, providing not just a diversion, but a connection that whispered to him, persistently, to stay...to fight...to live.

In the shared silences and unspoken understandings, Steven found a space where his struggles were neither trivialized nor magnified into defining characteristics. The players, each embroiled in their own silent battles, became inadvertent saviors, creating a lifeline fashioned out of empathy, resilience, and a shared escape that poker provided.

My friendship with Steven unfolded into a poignant reminder of the unspoken potency housed within our poker community. Every card dealt, every pot won or lost, and every friendly banter that danced around the table, had unwittingly become threads of a safety net, catching individuals like Steven when they teetered precariously on the edge.

His story has since become a silent fuel, driving my efforts to promote poker as not merely a game, but a subtle, yet profoundly impactful, therapeutic tool. Steven's journey, interspersed with both visible and invisible battles, mirrors the stories of countless others, subtly narrating tales of salvation found in unexpected places and friendships forged in the unlikeliest of circumstances.

In the echo of shuffled decks and chips being stacked, stories like Steven's whisper, silently affirming the healing, the camaraderie, and the unspoken understanding that every dealt hand fosters, nurturing not just a game, but a lifeline, quietly saving warriors in their unseen battles, every day.

The cards shuffled and chips clicked rhythmically in the background, but my mind was working through a different kind of strategy, beyond the immediate game at hand. My experiences, interwoven with the impactful narratives of individuals like Steven and countless others, illuminated a path that beckoned to be tread upon. A path that sought to marry the seemingly disparate worlds of poker and healing into a cohesive tapestry of therapeutic intervention and community building.

Moving forward, my vision for utilizing poker as a therapeutic tool is expansive and layered, aiming to reach as many individuals as possible and envelop them within the restorative embrace of the poker community. I envision creating a structured program where the principles of poker are employed as viable coping strategies, a tangible medium through which individuals can explore, understand, and subsequently, navigate their mental and emotional landscapes.

My plans involve developing workshops and programs that employ poker as a medium to enhance mental agility, foster social interaction, and provide a structured environment that facilitates emotional expression and management. These programs would be designed with the flexibility to cater to diverse groups of individuals, adapting to varied needs and contexts, while consistently providing a safe and supportive space for exploration and healing.

In partnership with veteran organizations, mental health advocates, and professionals within the psychological and psychiatric fields, I seek to create a bridge between the world of poker and mental health support. Through collaborations, we can create platforms that not only elevate awareness regarding the therapeutic potential of poker but also work towards integrating it into broader mental health initiatives and interventions.

Creating a network of "Poker Therapy Groups" across the country, and potentially, around the globe, is a tangible goal within this vision. These groups, underlined by principles of mutual respect, support, and confidentiality, would serve as safe havens for individuals to not only indulge in the game but also to share, connect, and find solace within a community that understands and empathizes with their journey.

Moreover, I aspire to establish a non-profit organization, dedicated to utilizing poker as a tool for mental and emotional well-being. This entity would work towards research, development, and implementation of poker-centric therapeutic interventions, while also serving as a hub for advocacy, awareness, and support for individuals finding healing and community through the game.

Through online platforms, I intend to create virtual spaces that extend the reach of these initiatives, ensuring that the healing power of poker is accessible to individuals beyond geographical constraints. Webinars, online workshops, and virtual poker therapy groups could cater to those who might be unable to access in-person programs, ensuring that the community and support are accessible to all who seek it.

In a world where mental and emotional struggles often remain shrouded in shadows and stigma, poker emerges as an unassuming yet potent light, providing direction, connection, and healing in its unique, subtle way. And as I chart the course forward, it is this light that I seek to amplify, ensuring it reaches every darkened corner, whispering hope and community to all who need it.

Through cards and chips, strategies and bluffs, friendships and support, my journey continues, shuffling, dealing, and playing it forward, one hand at a time.

"In the cards and the chaos, there's a sanctuary of strategy, a fellowship forged in the unpredictable sway of every dealt hand. Within these realms of risk and reward, we discover not just the means to navigate our traumas, but a community of hearts, steadfast and understanding, ever-ready to stand alongside us in every fold and fortune." – An Anonymous Cardplayer

This heartfelt reflection encapsulates the duality of poker as both a challenge and a solace, blending the art of the game with the human need for connection and understanding, especially in the journey through healing from trauma and embracing a future of possibilities.

CHAPTER 10

THE WINNING HAND: CONCLUDING THOUGHTS

As the familiar hum of shuffled cards and chiming chips enveloped me, a reflective tranquility washed over my spirit. It's almost surreal, pondering upon the undulating journey that unfolded across the verdant plains of poker tables, from clandestine rooms to the vibrant, bustling spaces of esteemed casinos. My relationship with poker, however, extended far beyond the walls where games were held, permeating deeply into my everyday life and in my struggles with Post-Traumatic Stress Disorder.

In every dealt hand, I discovered layers of myself previously buried beneath the turmoil of traumatic memories and numbing isolation. Poker, in its intricate blend of skill, luck, and social interaction, gradually became a solace, a mindful exercise enabling me to navigate the complex tapestry of emotions and thoughts that PTSD often entwines around one's psyche. It was within the sanctuary of this strategic game that I not only discovered avenues for mental tranquility but also serendipitously stumbled upon a community, diverse yet bound by a shared understanding, compassion, and an unwavering support that often eludes formal settings.

Yet, it's vital to acknowledge the ongoing journey; healing is not a finite destination but a continual path that we tread, with its own ebbs and flows. The haunting spectres of my experiences in the battlefield may never fully dissipate, and I accept that reality with a somber respect. Poker has neither erased nor diminished the gravity of those memories, but it has facilitated a mechanism through which I can explore, understand, and manage them, providing a cognitive and emotional outlet that is both therapeutic and engaging.

And there's a parallel story running alongside my own - a story echoed by countless others who have found solace, camaraderie, and a peculiar form of therapy upon the felt of the poker table. My aspirations and advocacies stem from these interspersed narratives, weaving together a tapestry that symbolizes hope, resilience, and a collective solidarity in navigating the murky waters of mental health challenges.

Looking towards the future, my vision is to intertwine the worlds of poker and mental health advocacy more cohesively. By sharing my journey and amplifying the voices of others who've found respite in the game, I hope to explore and perhaps, in some measure, demystify the therapeutic potential residing within this card game. Uniting mental health professionals, veteran organizations, and the poker community, I yearn to create a space where we can explore, understand, and utilize poker not merely as a game but as a tool - a medium through which we navigate our internal battles, forging ahead towards a future where our mental well-being is prioritized and nourished.

The journey of advocacy is akin to poker in many respects - it demands persistence, strategic thought, and an intrinsic understanding of the landscapes we navigate. It is not devoid of challenges, yet within those challenges, lies the potential for change, growth, and a progressive future where mental health is not shrouded in stigmas, but discussed, explored, and addressed openly and constructively.

In every chip stacked, in every card dealt, and in every hand played, may we find not just a game, but a reflection of our collective resilience, our shared empathy, and our unwavering hope towards a future where healing is not a solitary journey, but a collective endeavor, wrapped within the folds of understanding, strategy, and a heartfelt camaraderie.

And so, the cards continue to be dealt, the chips continue to stack, and we continue to play - understanding that every hand is not merely a bid for victory, but a shared moment in time, where we find understanding, solace, and a communal strength that propels us forward, always forward, into the enigmatic yet hopeful future that awaits. As I took my seat at the unofficial final table of the 2022 WSOP Super Turbo Bounty event, a potpourri of emotions cascaded through my soul. There, amidst the mingling murmurs and palpable excitement of the observers and fellow players, I found my hands instinctively shuffling my chips, a rhythmic dance that subtly steadied the cadence of my heartbeat.

My fingers, seasoned by countless hands and numerous tables, gracefully fanned the two cards dealt to me. A King of Diamonds and a Queen of Hearts. A courtly pair that held the potential for victory, yet masked behind their royal facades, lay the unpredictability of fate and luck. My mind, once cluttered by the tumultuous storms of PTSD, now found a peaceful enclave amidst the seemingly chaotic confluence of numbers, probabilities, and human behaviors unfolding before me.

Betting rounds passed in a cinematic blur, with chips cascading into the pot, each representing a tangible commitment, a chosen path within the labyrinthine journey of the hand. The Flop, a tangible cascade of hope and potentiality, revealed the Ten of Diamonds, Jack of Spades, and Ace of Hearts. A straight materialized before me, yet within its linear predictability, I found myself drifting into the abyss of memories and reflections.

There I was, encapsulated within a moment of triumphant potentiality, yet I found my thoughts wandering through the meandering pathways of my journey thus far. Every calculated risk at the poker table mirrored the innumerable decisions and actions throughout my life and military service, each culminating in both visible and invisible scars that became interwoven within my very being.

The Turn and the River, the Nine of Clubs and the Nine of Spades respectively, did little to quench the ascending tide of adrenaline and vulnerability enveloping the table and my consciousness. An opponent, with eyes gleaming with a subtle yet discernible amalgam of excitement and trepidation, pushed his stack forward, an all-in that beckoned a decision, a path to be chosen amidst the converging roads of risk and safety.

My chips followed suit, sliding gracefully into the burgeoning pot, each representing more than mere currency or a step towards victory. They symbolized the multifaceted journey of healing, the intertwining threads of pain, resilience, community, and newfound understanding that had become emblematic of my poker journey.

I revealed my cards, their faces exposing not only my hand but a vulnerability, a willingness to embrace the duality of loss and victory, pain and healing. My opponent's cards, the Ace of Diamonds and Ace of Spades, though victorious in their conventional strength, were met not with disappointment or desolation on my part, but a serene acceptance, a recognition of the transient nature of both poker and life.

Despite the dwindling stack before me, and the eventual 10th place finish, I found within that hand, within that moment of loss, an unspoken victory, an ode to the resilience and transformative power encapsulated within the realm of poker and life's perpetual journey.

In the royal figures of my final hand, amidst the intoxicating blend of triumph and defeat, I saw not an end, but a continuity, a narrative that extends beyond the felt of the poker table, permeating every facet of my existence and my ongoing battle with PTSD.

It was a reminder that our strongest hands, our most vivid victories, are not always etched within the moments of conventional success, but often reside within our capacity to navigate loss, to find meaning and strength within the ebb and flow of life's inexorable tides, and to emerge not unscathed, but undeterred, perpetually propelled forward by the very currents that seek to hinder us.
In the serene dimness of the room, I stare at the worn cards before me, every scratch and bend whispering tales from numerous poker tables. They cradle within them an unseen, yet profoundly felt, healing power that has guided my vessel through the tumultuous seas of PTSD towards shores of tranquility and acceptance.

I remember the inception, where the turbulence of war lingered, a haunting specter within the recesses of my mind, where sleep was perpetually marred by the resurgence of memories too painful to articulate, too vivid to dissipate into the abyss of forgetfulness.

Poker emerged, not merely as a game, but a lighthouse amidst the engulfing darkness, a medium through which I could navigate the internal chaos, redirecting the mental and emotional energies into calculations, strategies, and, most poignantly, connections. The tables became arenas, not just of competition, but of shared humanity, where beneath the veiled faces of stoic poker players, lay threads of understanding, unspoken yet palpably felt.

As the cards were shuffled and hands were dealt, I found within the numbers and faces, metaphors that transcended the materiality of the game. Every fold mirrored a surrender, not to defeat, but to acceptance, understanding that not every battle waged within need be fought. Every raise embodied a stand, a declaration of presence in the face of adversity, both at the table and within the mind. And every call symbolized a continuation, a decision to proceed despite the unseen, to embrace the unknown paths that lay veiled before me.

With every hand played, with every individual met at the tables, I gleaned fragments of wisdom, shards of understanding that gradually coalesced into a holistic image of healing, growth, and perpetual resilience. The voices, once solitary echoes within, found harmonies in the stories and experiences shared amidst bets, bluffs, and folds.

The poker tables became sanctuaries where, amidst the game's inherent unpredictability and competition, I unearthed a consistent, unwavering source of camaraderie, challenge, and, fundamentally, a restoration of self not defined by the traumas of the past, but illuminated by a present and future crafted by newfound understanding, compassion, and an unyielding flame of resilience.

As I navigate this ongoing journey, the game continues to cradle my progression, not as an escape, but a therapeutic ally, persistently revealing that beneath the visages of stoic poker faces and concealed hands, resides an indomitable human spirit, perpetually seeking, growing, and playing forward towards a future unshackled from the chains of trauma. It's a peaceful rebellion against the internal and external wars, a quiet assertion that even amidst the chaos, there is a place for joy, for community, and for one's self to be whole again. Poker, in its enigmatic beauty, has become an unexpected, yet deeply cherished, vessel towards that holistic serenity.

"Perseverance is not a long race; it's many short races one after the other." - Walter Elliot

In every short race symbolized by a hand of poker, in every decision made at the table, and in each person met along this incredible journey, perseverance has been the undercurrent, propelling forward amidst the unpredictable tides of life and the mind. Walter Elliot's words echo deeply, a reminder that persistence, in every small moment, every shared smile across the poker table, and every shared story of triumph and despair, crafts a resilient path forward, allowing healing and growth to perpetually unfold.

APPENDIX

Appendix A: Resources for Learning Poker

1. Books:
   - "Super/System" by Doyle Brunson
   - "Harrington on Hold'em" by Dan Harrington
   - "The Theory of Poker" by David Sklansky

2. Websites and Online Platforms:
   - [PokerStars School](https://www.pokerstarsschool.com/)
   - [Upswing Poker](https://upswingpoker.com/)
   - [TwoPlusTwo Forums](https://forumserver.twoplustwo.com/)

3. Local Clubs and Groups:
   - [Meetup: Poker Nights](https://www.meetup.com/)
   - Various casino poker rooms and local charity events

Appendix B: PTSD Support Resources and Contacts

A critical section providing a range of support options for individuals struggling with PTSD, ensuring that readers are aware of the professional and community resources available to them.

1. Helplines:
   - National Suicide Prevention Lifeline: 1-800-273-TALK (8255)

- Veterans Crisis Line: 1-800-273-8255 (Press 1)

2. Websites and Online Support:
   - [National Center for PTSD](https://www.ptsd.va.gov/)
   - [PTSD Foundation of America](http://ptsdusa.org/)
   - [Sidran Traumatic Stress Institute](https://www.sidran.org/)

3. Support Groups:
   - [Find a PTSD Support Group Near You](https://www.mentalhealthamerica.net/find-support-groups)
   - [Online PTSD Support Group](https://www.myptsd.com/)

ABOUT THE AUTHOR

Shaun Colquhoun is not just an author; he's a testament to resilience, adaptability, and the human spirit's unwavering strength. With a past deeply rooted in the demanding terrains of Afghanistan and a present anchored in the intricate world of poker tables, Shaun's journey is both unique and universally resonant.

His experiences as a soldier provided him with insights into the profound depths of human emotions–courage, fear, camaraderie, and loss. These experiences, while scarring, also became the foundation upon which Shaun built his subsequent journey of healing and discovery. The world of poker, with its mix of strategy, intuition, and human connection, became an unexpected sanctuary for Shaun, offering both an escape from and a way to process the traumas of his past.

In this book, Shaun invites readers into his world, sharing not only the harrowing realities of war and PTSD but also the therapeutic power of poker, an unconventional yet transformative healing path. Through his narrative, he hopes to inspire, educate, and perhaps offer a new perspective on the ways we can cope, heal, and eventually thrive.

Off the pages, Shaun continues to be an advocate for mental health, emphasizing the importance of finding one's unique path to healing and the power of community and connection in that journey. His story is a reminder that even in the most challenging moments, there's always a hand worth playing, and sometimes, the game itself can be a beacon of hope.

Made in the USA
Las Vegas, NV
06 June 2024

90811004R00057